90 RECIPES

from the

IONA COMMUNITY

Edited by SUE PATTISON

90 WHOLESOME AND INEXPENSIVE RECIPES
MANY OF WHICH USE PULSES AND CEREALS
AS A MAJOR SOURCE OF PROTEIN

wild goose publications

First Published 1986

Further information about the fund raising campaign for the MacLeod Centre may be had from The Director, The MacLeod Centre Appeal, 23 Learmonth Terrace, Edinburgh EH4 1PG Telephone: (031) 332 7636

WILD GOOSE PUBLICATIONS

The wild goose is a Celtic symbol of the Holy Spirit.
It serves as the logo of Iona Community Publications.

Pearce Institute, 840 Govan Road,
GLASGOW   G51 3UT

☎   (041) 445 4561

Printed in Great Britain by
Antony Rowe Ltd, Chippenham, Wiltshire

90 Recipes From The Iona Community represents the efforts of all its contributors towards the *Go 90* Appeal to raise £800,000 to build the MacLeod Centre on Iona. I am deeply indebted to them all. The MacLeod Centre will be the Iona Community's new Youth Centre, a major aim being to build a centre for the promotion of Peace, both individually, corporately and internationally.

In this context it is fitting, therefore, that our contributors have furnished us with wholesome, inexpensive recipes, many of which use pulses and cereals as a major cource of protein. This reflects our awareness that it takes far less land and far fewer resources to raise vegetable protein than animal protein. We are aware today that food — its production, distribution and consumption — is a highly political commodity, and we can express our awareness and concern in the way we plan our diets. Yet there will always be a place for food as an expression of joy and celebration, and recipes will be found in these pages for such occasions too.

The recipes reflect both traditional Scottish food and also far-flung influences. Wherever possible I have named contributors and where they live. They represent members, spouses, associates and friends of the Iona Community, and therefore reflect also its geographical spread, for we are a community inspired by Iona, but few of us are resident there.

As we who have contributed share these recipes with all who will use them, let us together remember the Celtic Rune of Hospitality:

> I saw a stranger yestreen,
> I put food in the eating place,
> Drink in the drinking place,
> Music in the listening place,
> And in the name of the TRIUNE,
> He blessed myself and my house,
> My cattle and my dear ones,
> And the lark said in her song
>   often often often
> Goes the CHRIST in the stranger's guise.

Sue Pattison,
Editor.
Sept. '86

Grateful thanks to:

All the contributors of the Recipes
and Valerie Yule for the Illustrations.

4

SECTION SIX - CEREALS

SECTION SEVEN - SALADS

SECTION EIGHT - SWEETS

SECTION NINE - BISCUITS AND CAKES

SECTION TEN - MISCELLANEOUS

Abbreviations used in the Recipes

dssp.	=	Dessertspoon
fl.oz.	=	Fluid ounce
g.	=	gram
hr.	=	Hour
Kg.	=	Kilogram
lb.	=	Pound
Marg.	=	Margarine
Mins.	=	Minutes
oz.	=	Ounce
pt.	=	Pint
qt.	=	Quart
S.R.	=	Self raising
sq.in.	=	Square inch
tbsp.	=	Tablespoon
tsp.	=	Teaspoon

At the foot of each Recipe the letters F.G. refer to the Family Group of which the contributor is a member

1

CARROT AND POTATO SOUP

1 lb. carrots	Bouquet garni
8 oz. potatoes	Sea Salt
1 large onion finely chopped	Freshly ground black pepper
1 oz. butter or margarine	2 tbsp. Worcestershire sauce
1½ pts. stock	1 tbsp. tomato puree

2 tbsp. chopped parsley

Finely chop the carrots. Peel and finely chop the potatoes. Melt the butter in a saucepan on a low heat. Stir in the carrots, potatoes and onion. Cover and let them sweat for 10 mins. Pour in the stock and bring to the boil. Add bouquet garni and season well. Cover and simmer for 20 mins. Remove the bouquet garni. Put half the soup into a blender with the Worcestershire sauce and tomato puree and work until smooth. Stir into the rest of the soup and add the chopped parsley.

Serves 4 people.

Anonymous, Glasgow.

2

CUCUMBER SOUP

1 peeled cucumber roughly chopped	1 carrot
1 chopped onion	1 tsp. curry powder
1½ pts. liquid (stock)	2 chicken cubes
1½ tbsp. cornflour	½ pt. milk.

Sauté the cucumber, carrot, onion and curry powder. Add the liquid (stock) and chicken cubes. Simmer till cooked (½hr.). Mash or liquidise. Add the cornflour blended with the milk.

Ruby Crawford, Fife Family Group

3

GROUNDNUT SOUP (GAMBIA)

25 g. oil	50 g. flour
850 ml. chicken stock	120 g. Crunchy Peanut Butter
1 tsp. tomato puree	Salt, pepper, cayenne to season.

Make a paste with the oil and flour, add the tomato puree, seasons and peanut butter. Gradually add the stock, stirring all the time. Simmer for 20-25 mins. If liked some cream can be stirred in just before serving.

Liz Paterson, Airdrie

4   LENTILS, MONASTERY STYLE - SOUP FOR 4 - 6

In large pot sauté 3 - 5 mins: ¼ cup olive (or any) oil
                                   2 large onions, chopped
                                   1 carrot, chopped

Add and sauté 1 min. more: ½ tsp. each of dried thyme & marjoram

Add: 3 cups stock or seasoned water
                                  1 cup dry lentils, washed
                                  salt to taste
                                  ¼ cup chopped fresh parsley
                                  1 lb. canned tomatoes

Cook in covered pot until lentils are tender (about 45 mins.)
     and add: ¼ cup sherry

Have ready: 2/3 cup grated cheese

To serve: place 2 tbsp. grated cheese in each bowl and top with soup

          Especially delicious served with corn muffins.

This was my staple diet as a student! Easy and quick to make in the
pressure cooker. (The sherry was an optional extra for high days and
holidays). Flatmates soon mastered the basic recipe and everyone
developed their own variations. It usually began life as a thick main
course and a few days later was more like a consommé! The recipe was
given to me by Michelle, a New Zealander who was cook in the Abbey the
summer of '76.

P.S. I've never had it with corn muffins!

                                        Catherine Hepburn, Central F.G.

5   YOUTH CAMP NETTLE SOUP

Fresh young nettles: Pick with rubber gloves enough nettles to fill
the soup pot twice. Wash and remove any thick stalks.

          1 onion, chopped   1 litre stock
          Salt and pepper   25 g. marg.
                         50 g. flour

Cook the nettles in the stock along with the seasoning and onion till
tender (about 20 mins.). Make a roux with the flour and marg.
Liquidise the nettles and add to the roux, return to the heat and
bring through the boil, check seasoning and serve.

                                        Liz Paterson, Airdrie

8

PEAS BROSE

3 Dessertspoons Peas Meal	1 nugget butter or marg.
1 Dessertspoon sugar	Pinch salt

Boiling water

Place peas meal in a bowl. Add marg., sugar and salt. Pour on the boiling water slowly, stirring all the time, till a soft consistency is reached. Serve with milk or cream.

Cameron Wallace, Greenock F.G.

HINTS

Soups From Stock

Use all left over vegetable water - add:

T.V.P.
Oats
Flavourings such as marmite, herbs.
odd vegetables and/or mushrooms to suit taste

Lisbet Rutter, Edinburgh.

7   ACHARD DE LEGUMES

1 cauliflower	1 cabbage
1 lb. French beans	1 lb. carrots
1 lb. small onions	a few chillies (to taste)
1 oz. mustard seeds	2 level tbsp. turmeric
1 head of garlic (or to taste)	or saffron powder
½ pt. vinegar	1 oz. root ginger
1 pt. cooking oil	Salt to taste

Wash and cut into fine strips the cauliflower, cabbage, French beans,
and carrots. Blanch, drain and put into the sun on a tray for at least
three hours until the vegetables are dry.
Sauce: Mix turmeric with 3 tbsp. vinegar. In a large saucepan heat the
oil gently, then add the turmeric mixture. Cook 5 mins. Add the
onions, sliced lengthways, add the chillies sliced in 4 lengthways and
without seeds, then add the garlic, ginger and mustard crushed
together. Cook 3 - 4 mins. Remove from heat, add the vegetables and
mix well. Leave until quite cool and put into jars. Keeps well.

You can vary the spices and vegetables according to taste and what is
available and cheap. Eat with cold meat, cheese, on it's own in bread,
with almost any cooked dish. Very good addition to any sandwich!

Liz Crosby, Mauritius

8   CHUNKY CARROTS & PARSNIPS IN CURRY SAUCE

1 lb. carrots (1½ inch rings)	2 oz. marg.
1 lb. parsnips (1½ inch chunks)	2 level tbsp. flour
1 level tbsp. mild curry powder	2 oz. sultanas
1 veg. stock cube crumbled	1 tbsp. lemon juice
salt, pepper	5 oz. natural yoghurt
1 medium cooking apple peeled, cored and chopped	

Parboil the carrots for 10 mins. Pour off water and make it up to ½pt.
with tap water - reserve. Melt the marg. in a pan and fry the onion
gently for 2 - 3 mins. Add the carrots and parsnips, continue frying
for 2 mins. Stir occasionally. Add the flour and curry powder and cook
2 mins. Add the apple, sultanas, stock cube and reserved liquid plus
lemon juice and seasoning. Must keep stirring or it will stick. Bring
to the boil, cover pan and simmer on low heat 40 - 45 mins. stirring
occasionally until vegetables are soft and sauce has thickened. Before
serving, stir in yoghurt. Serve with hot brown rice. (Rinse well, 2oz.
dried rice per person. Do not add salt to water as it hardens the
grain - if required use at end of cooking or use lemon juice instead).

Serves 4

Mary Robins, Glasgow

COURGETTE QUICHE

Preparation time: One hour/fifteen mins.   Cooking time: 35-40 mins.

                1 wholemeal flour pastry crust recipe
                3 - 4 medium sized courgettes (zucchini)
        6 oz. natural yoghurt   4 eggs
        4 oz. cheddar cheese (grated) 1 oz. milk
        1 oz. parmesan cheese (grated) 1 tbsp. basil
        ½ tsp. ground black pepper   1 tsp. salt
                1 small onion

Step one: One hour before main preparation time (about two hours before you want to eat!) wash, and shred or grate the courgettes (zucchini). Mix the basil, salt and shredded courgette in a bowl and leave to stand for an hour.

Step two: Drain the liquid off the shredded courgette, and put the latter in a skillet with chopped up onion and a small amount of cooking oil. Simmer gently to soften up the vegetables - a few mins. should do.

Meanwhile line a 10 inch quiche dish with the rolled out pastry crust. Prick base and weigh down with beans or blind cooking weights or whatever you normally use, and bake for 8 mins. with oven at 350°F. Mix eggs, yoghurt, milk and pepper in another bowl.

Step three: Take the pastry case out of the oven, line the bottom with half the grated cheddar cheese, top with half the courgette and onion mix, sprinkle with the parmesan cheese, add the rest of the vegetable mix, and pour in the egg/milk/yoghurt mixture. Top with the rest of the grated cheddar cheese and bake in the oven for 35 - 40 mins. or until set and turning golden brown on top.

Serve with salad, baked potatoes.

This dish keeps well in fridge or freezer.

                                        Anna Briggs, Toronto

10   SPINACH AND CHEESE

Make Roux. Add 1 tin, or equivalent fresh, cooked and well drained, (preferably chopped) spinach and stir in well. Add one egg and stir in well. Re-heat and serve with grated cheese and potatoes.

                    Serves 3 - 4

                                        Lisbett Rutter, Edinburgh

MARROW CROUTADE

4 oz. ground hazelnuts	4 oz. wholemeal breadcrumbs
1 tsp. mixed herbs	1 crushed clove of garlic
1 oz. marg.	1 lb. diced marrow
1 onion (finely chopped)	3 skinned tomatoes (chopped)
1 tbsp. parmesan grated cheese	Pepper (& salt if desired)

A little cooking oil

Base: Mix together the nuts and breadcrumbs. Put 3 oz. of this mixture to one side for the topping. Add the herbs to the rest and rub in the marg. Press into base of a 7in. dish and bake for 20 mins. @ 200°C.

Filling: Gently fry the onion and garlic in a small amount of cooking oil. Add the diced marrow until soft at the edges then finally the chopped tomato and pepper. Stir until the marrow is coated with tomato then pile on top of the base.

Topping: Add the parmesan cheese to the breadcrumb mixture set aside earlier. Smooth this on top of the marrow filling. Bake for 20 - 25 mins. in oven @ 200°C.

N.B. This is delicious with a creamed mushroom filling.

We like to serve this with a cheese filled jacket potato.

Pat Welburn, North East England F.G.

RAT(ATOUILLE)

(My favourite recipe for lazy people;
The quantities aren't important, nor is the cooking time!)

Aubergines	Courgettes
Peppers (red, green, yellow)	Onions
Mushrooms	Tomatoes (tinned or fresh)

Herbs - basil, oregano

Method: Wash the veg. and de-seed the peppers. Chop, dice, slice and cube the veg. Throw into a large casserole dish and add the herbs. Place in a low oven for a few hours until it is all cooked.

Serve: With grated cheese and lots of good brown bread.

Comments: Use seasonal vegetables when cheap. Often stores will sell off slightly old, damaged vegetables which make this dish even cheaper.

Barbara Quigley, Glasgow East F.G.

SPINACH ROULADE

1¼ lb. fresh spinach (broccoli could be used as a substitute)

4 eggs, separated   Pinch of nutmeg
Salt and pepper   8 oz. cottage cheese

Preheat oven to gas mark 6, 400°F (200°C). Wash the spinach and shake off excess water. Put in a pan and cook quickly for 6 - 8 mins. (or boil broccoli until soft and then drain). Liquidise. Mix the egg yolks with the liquidised spinach and season with salt and pepper and nutmeg. Whisk the egg whites until they form soft peaks. Stir just 1 tbsp. of egg whites into the spinach mixture and then fold in the remainder in two batches. Put the mixture into a swiss roll tin 8" x 12" lined with greaseproof paper and bake for 10 - 15 mins. until beginning to brown.

When cooked take it out of the oven and turn it out onto a clean sheet of greaseproof paper - remove the backing paper. Roll up the mixture, with the new greaseproof paper between, as in a swiss roll and leave to cool.

When cool, unroll, remove the greaseproof paper and spread the cottage cheese onto the spinach and then re-roll. Serve with green salad and new potatoes.

Lynda Wright, Lochaber F.G.

VEGETABLE CASSEROLE

2 tbsp. sunflower oil   1 large onion - chopped
3 sticks celery - chopped   3 carrots - thinly sliced
14 oz. can tomatoes   2 tbsp. tomato pureé
¼ pt. good stock   4 oz. button mushrooms
        1 small cauliflower - broken into florets
        15 oz. can red kidney beans - drained
                 Salt and pepper

Heat the oil in a saucepan and quickly fry the onion, celery and carrot until beginning to brown. Stir in the tomatoes, pureé, stock, seasoning and beans. Cover with a lid and simmer for 20 mins. until carrot is tender. Then add the cauliflower and mushrooms and cook for a further 5 mins.

Serve with grated cheese on top for added protein. Good as a vegetable accompaniment or as a supper dish with garlic bread.

Hilda Lang, Glasgow West F.G.

15   VEGETARIAN COTTAGE PIE

Filling: Tin red kidney beans - drained (or equivalent)
      1 onion - chopped   2 small carrots - finely grated
      1 tbsp. marmite   1 cup tomato juice (or water)
      Flour to thicken   Seasoning to taste

Topping:
      Mashed potato   Cheese if wished

Filling: Mix all the ingedients except the flour in a pan and simmer
for about 10 mins. Remove from heat. Add flour in a little of the
water (or tomato juice). Stir quickly and return to heat to thicken.
Put into a casserole dish.
Cover with the mashed potato. Top with cheese if required.
Cook in a hot oven for 15 mins.

           Annie Delahunty, South Wales F.G.

16   VEGETABLE SAMOSAS

(Strictly for convenience cooks!)

1 small packet flaky pastry - vegetarian   Oil, vegetable marg.
1 small packet of stir fry vegetables   2 tbsp. tomato ketchup
           1 tsp. curry powder

Heat oil and marg. in a small pan. Preheat oven (see pastry pack for
details) Gas 7. Add vegetables to the pan and cook quickly to retain
crispness and flavour. Remove from heat. Add ketchup and curry powder
and blend well. Roll out pastry to ½inch thickness. Cut into squares.
Place a tsp. of mixture on each square. Seal the edges with a little
water. Slit the tops with a knife. Place on a greased baking sheet.
Cook for 15 - 20 mins. until crisp and brown.

Perfect as a starter or for unexpected guests.   Makes 9 - 10

           Mary Robins, Glasgow

HINTS

Vegetarian Toad in the Hole

Use any 'Toad in the Hole' recipe, but instead of sausages use:
      pre-cooked onions   and/or soft (over-ripe) tomatoes
      and/or pre-cooked carrots   herbs as liked
           some grated cheese

Gardeners Pie

As 'Shepherds Pie'
      but instead of meat use mixed cooked vegetables (drained)

           Lisbett Rutter, Edinburgh

17   KEDGEREE

(I used this a great deal as a student and it was always enjoyed –
        not elaborate, but filling and flexible)
      (for two hungry people – or as many as you like)

  Rice, brown or long grain – 1 cupful before cooking
  Fish – 2 small smoked fillets or small tin of mackerel or tuna
      or larger quantity of fish scraps
  Eggs – 2 (or more)
  Milk – enough to cook fish in
  Salt, pepper, curry powder to taste

Boil rice, meanwhile cook or reheat the fish in milk and hardboil the
eggs (these can share the rice pan if space or water is short). Drain
the rice and add the cooked flaked fish, chopped hardboiled eggs, and
the milk in which the fish was cooked. Season to taste – a little
curry powder lifts it out of the realm of the mundane into the realm
of the tasty!

                     Margaret Stewart, Edinburgh West F.G.

18   PASTA WITH TUNA

Cook pasta (long or short) as usual, till ready if dish is to be
served at once, or for about half the time if the dish is to be
reheated or left in the oven for several hours.

Sauce: Tuna – 1 tin serves 2 – 3 portions
           or 5 – 6 if "lengthened" with a pint of white sauce.

Soften the tuna, stirring over a gentle heat in its own oil, adding a
little milk, or the white sauce. Flavour with salt and plenty of black
pepper. Add   capers   if   liked,   or   anchovies   and/or   garlic
granules/salt.

Stir into pasta and serve, or put into a slow oven, either with a lid
on or a topping of cheese and breadcrumbs.

                     Violet Ross, Tayside F.G.

19 TUNA PIE

Small tin of tuna fish   6 cream crackers
3 eggs beaten with a little milk   Seasoning

Drain oil from the tuna. Crumble the crackers and mix them with the
tuna. Add the egg mixture. Place in an ovenproof dish without a lid
and bake for about 20 mins. on Gas mark 4 or 300°F.

Ella Ferguson, Kings Park Church, Glasgow

20 TUNA AND YOGHURT QUICHE

(This is an ideal quiche for those who, like me, always produce pastry
cases with cracks in - as the mixture does not seep through!)

One 7" pastry case, baked blind, wholemeal if possible
7 oz. tin tuna fish   5 oz. yoghurt
2 eggs   4 oz. grated cheese
Salt and pepper   1 tbsp. capers (optional)

Mash the tuna, mix with the yoghurt and beaten eggs. Season to taste
and pour into the pastry case. Sprinkle cheese on top. Bake in a slow
to moderate oven for 20 - 30 mins. until the filling has set.

Win Kennedy, South Midlands F.G.

21 THE WOODCOCK FISH SPECIAL

4 Pieces of cod or haddock
4 eggs (2 or 3 if you're not an "Egg Fan"!!)
1 oz. marg.   Salt and pepper
1 oz. plain flour   ¼ pt. milk
               4 oz. grated cheese

1. Brush the fish with a little cooking oil and grill for 5 - 8 mins.
2. Hard boil the eggs, shell and slice.
3. Place the fish in a well greased dish and add the sliced eggs.
4. Make up a cheese sauce with the remaining ingredients and pour
   over the fish and eggs.
5. Put into the oven at Regulo 3 - 4 (350 - 375°F) for 15 - 20 mins.

Sheila Woodcock, London East F.G.

16

4 Rashers streaky bacon	1 cooking apple
4 slices wholewheat bread	Butter or marg.

4 tbsp. chutney

Cut rind from the bacon. Cut each rasher in half crossways. Quarter and core the apple and cut into 16 lengthwise slices. Toast the slices of bread on one side only. Turn the slices over, lightly butter and spread with chutney. Lay 4 apple slices on each slice of toast. Put the toast back under the grill for 2 mins. so the apples begin to soften. Grill the pieces of bacon and put them on top of the apples.

Serves 4 people

Anonymous, Glasgow

23   HOMESTEAD LOAF

2 Slices brown bread	2 medium carrots
1 large cooking apple	Rind of one lemon
1 medium sized onion	8 oz. sausagemeat
4 oz. oat meal	2 level tsp. salt
1 level tsp. pepper,	1 level tsp. marg.
1 level tsp. sage	½ level tsp. mixed spice
1 egg	Chutney to glaze

Make bread into breadcrumbs and put in a large bowl. Add grated carrots, grated apple, grated lemon rind and finely chopped onion. Add the rest of the ingredients and mix well.

Brush a 1lb. loaf tin with oil. Spoon in the mixture and press down. Place tin on a baking tray. Spoon 2 tbsp. of fat (preferably from chicken) over the mixture and bake for one hour at No.4 or 350°F.

To serve: Turn out onto a warm dish and glaze with the chutney.

Good on its own or with chicken.

Hilda Lang, Glasgow West F.G.

BEEFY LAYER LOAF

1 packet parsley and thyme stuffing mix

1 large onion	1½ lb. minced beef
1 heaped tsp. horseradish relish	1 dssp. Worcester sauce
1 heaped tbsp. tomato pureé	Salt and pepper to taste
1 beaten egg	4 heaped tbsp. fresh white breadcrumbs

Mix up the stuffing mix, leave to stand for 10 mins. Peel and finely chop the onion and put into a bowl with the mince, horseradish relish, worcester sauce, tomato pureé, salt and pepper. Add beaten egg and breadcrumbs and mix ingredients well. Press half the mixture into a well greased 2 lb. loaf tin. Cover with the prepared stuffing and finish with the remaining beef mixture. Press down firmly and cook in a hot oven for 1 hour at 220°C (425°F) Gas 7.

Morag Boffey, Greenock F.G.

HOT CHICKEN SALAD

4 cups diced cooked chicken	1 red or green pepper, diced
1 onion, diced	1 cup red grated cheese
1 cup flaked almonds	4 hard boiled eggs, diced
2 cups celery, diced	Juice of large lemon

1 large bottle Helmans mayonnaise

Mix all the ingredients in a large bowl with the mayonnaise, until a good consistency. Leave overnight covered.

Eat cold - or, better still, before cooking sprinkle with plain salted potato crisps and cook in a large flat dish for one hour @ 200°C (400°F) Gas 6.

Serve with a green salad.

Morag Boffey, Greenock F.G.

COLD CHICKEN SOUFFLÉ

1½ oz. butter	1 oz. plain flour
½ pt. chicken stock	2 eggs, separated
3 tbsp. gelatine	2 tbsp. dry sherry
8 oz. cooked chicken, minced	1 oz. ham, minced
2 hard boiled eggs, chopped	Salt
¼ pt. double cream, lightly whipped.	Pepper

Garnish: 1 hard boiled egg, sliced   Chopped parsley

Prepare a 2pt. soufflé dish. Melt the butter in a saucepan, stir in the flour and cook for 1 min. Remove from heat and gradually blend in stock. Heat, stirring until sauce thickens. Simmer, stirring for 1 min. Cool slightly, then beat in the egg yolks.

Put water in a bowl and sprinkle gelatine over it. Place over a pan of hot water, mix in the sherry. Stir the gelatine, chicken, ham and hard boiled eggs into the sauce, then fold in the cream. Add salt and pepper. Whisk the egg whites until stiff and fold into the souffle mixture evenly. Turn into the soufflé dish and leave to cool. Then garnish.

Morag Boffey, Greenock F.G.

CHICKEN CASSEROLE

4 chicken portions	1 spanish onion
2 oz. butter	1 tbsp. oil
2 rounded tbsp. plain flour	¼ pt. chicken stock
Salt	Pepper

1 rounded tbsp. tomato pureé or tomato ketchup

Remove skin and bones from the chicken pieces. Peel and chop the onion. Heat the butter and oil in a pan and fry the chicken until brown all over. Transfer to a casserole dish. Add the chopped onion to pan and fry till lightly brown. Stir in the chicken stock, flour, tomato pureé and seasoning to taste. Bring to the boil and pour over the chicken.

Cover and cook for 1¼ hours in a moderate oven, Reg 4, 350°F or 180°C

Margaret M. McLagan, King's Park Church, Glasgow

28   MINESTRONE CHICKEN

4 chicken portions
1 packet minestrone soup   1 tsp. gravy powder

Skin the chicken portions and dust them with soup powder. Heat a little oil in a frying pan and seal the chicken pieces. Place the chicken in a casserole dish. Mix the remains of the soup powder and the gravy powder with ¼ pt. water. Pour over the chicken pieces and put the casserole in a moderate oven for at least an hour.

(This can also be cooked very slowly in a large frying-pan-with-lid on top of the cooker)

Serves 4

Mary Gordon, Edinburgh North F.G.

29   FRENCH KIDNEYS

1 lb. lamb or ox kidney   2 oz. plain flour
Salt and pepper   1 oz. butter
2 - 3 onions   Few cloves
Mushrooms (optional)   ¼ pt. water
Sherry

Wash, core and chop the kidneys. Roll the pieces in the flour and seasoning, then fry gently in butter for 5 mins. Add water, chopped onions, cloves (and mushrooms, if included), and cook over a low heat until the kidneys are tender. Keep an eye on the consistency of the sauce and add more water if it gets too thick.

Add sherry to taste just before serving.

Catherine Harkin, Ayrshire F.G.

30   LITTLE BIT DIFFERENT MINCE

1 lb. shoulder steak mince   ¼ lb. sweetcure bacon
1 thick slice wholemeal bread   2 tsp. finely chopped parsley
Pinch of salt and pepper

Mix together the minced steak, wholemeal breadcrumbs and chopped parsley, plus salt and pepper. Roll up tablespoons of mixture in slices of bacon. Place the mince and bacon 'parcels' in a casserole dish. Add 2 tbsp. water. Bake in a pre-heated oven, 180°C, 350°F, Reg 4 for 1 hour.

For party occasions, serve with a thick, creamy cheese sauce, lightly flavoured with basil.

Jessie Thomson, King's Park Church, Glasgow

1 tin cream of tomato soup
1 chopped onion
1 egg

1 lb. mince
Handful of dry rice (uncooked)
Seasoning

Put the mince in a bowl with the onion, rice, seasoning and egg to bind mixture together. Roll into balls and place in a casserole dish. Pour over it the tin of cream of tomato soup and bake in oven for 45 mins. @ Gas mark 4, 300°F.

Serve with cooked rice.

Ella Ferguson, King's Park Church, Glasgow

32   RICE AND PORK FRY

10 oz. long grain brown rice
8 oz. belly pork rashers
4 oz. boiling sausage
4 medium oranges

1 large onion, quartered and sliced
1 garlic clove, finely chopped
6 oz. tin sweetcorn, drained
1 tsp. paprika

1 tsp. cayenne pepper

Cook the rice in lightly salted boiling water for about 45 mins. or until tender. Drain, rinse with cold water and drain again. Cut the rind and any bones from the pork. Dice the rashers. Thinly slice the boiling sausage. Cut the rind and pith from the oranges. Cut each orange in half and thinly slice. Heat a large, heavy frying pan on a high heat with no fat. Put in the pork and stir until it browns. Lower the heat and add the onion, garlic and sliced sausage. Cook until the onion is soft. Mix in the rice and sweetcorn, paprika and cayenne pepper. Stir until rice has heated through. Mix in the pieces of orange and cook for 1 min. more.

Serve with a salad.

Anonymous, Glasgow

HINTS

To 'stretch' mince

Per ½ lb. of mince add a good handful of TVP and (if wanted) beef flavouring; and/or make soup and stir in mince; or start mince in minimal amount of water until it cooks in own fat. Add flour and stir, adding water if necessary.

Lisbett Rutter, Edinburgh

33   CARROT AND CHEESE SLICE

(Quick and Easy)

Mix together:

4 oz. grated cheese	6 oz. grated carrot
1 chopped onion	5 oz. oats
2 oz. melted marg.	Salt/pepper/herbs

1 beaten egg

Place on a buttered baking tray and heat in an oven for 20 mins. (190°C, 375°F)

Serve with parsley sauce.

Ruby Crawford, Fife F.G.

34   CHEESE AND LENTIL LOAF

6 oz. real lentils	12 fl.oz. water
4 oz. grated cheddar cheese	1 onion, peeled and finely chopped
1 tbsp. fresh parsley, chopped	¼ tsp. cayenne pepper
A little lemon juice	1 large egg
3 tbsp. single cream	Salt

Freshly ground black pepper

Pre-heat oven to gas mark 5, 375°F. Rinse and cook the lentils in a tightly covered pan with the water for 10 - 15 mins. Start with only a small amount of water and check after 10 mins. to see if you need to add more. The mixture should cook to a stiff pureé. Remove pan from the heat and put in the grated cheese, chopped onion, parsley, cayenne pepper and lemon juice. Season to taste.

In a separate bowl lightly beat the egg, stir in the cream and then pour this mixture over the lentils. Grease a 1lb loaf tin with the butter and press in the mixture. Bake for 45 - 50 mins. until the top is golden brown and the mixture feels firm to the touch. If you are serving it hot, let it stand for 10 mins. in the tin before turning it out.

Can be served with tomato sauce, baked potatoes and green vegetables, or with salad, or with fried rice and grilled tomatoes.

Serves 4

Jean and John Williams, Lichfield, Birmingham F.G.

CHEESE PUDDING

4 oz. breadcrumbs	4 oz. grated cheese
1 egg, beaten	2 oz. butter, melted
¼ pt. milk	

Worcester sauce, salt and pepper to taste

Warm the butter and milk together, pour over the crumbs and cheese, add seasoning and the egg.
Pour into an ovenproof dish and bake @ 375°F for 35 - 40 mins.

Catherine Harkin, Ayrshire F.G.

---

36   # LEEKY EGGS

8 oz. - 12 oz. leeks	4 eggs

Cheese sauce:	½ oz. low fat marg.	1 dssp. wholewheat flour
	½ pt. skimmed milk	3 oz. grated cheddar cheese

Wash and chop the leeks. Heat slowly in a pan with a very little oil. Simmer for 15 - 20 mins. Put the eggs in a pan of cold water and bring to the boil for 10 mins. Put the sauce ingredients in a pan and bring to the boil, stirring all the time (add cheese when boiling). Drain the leeks and put in the bottom of an ovenproof dish. Arrange the hard boiled eggs in halves on leeks. Pour sauce over and brown under a grill.

(N.B. Leeks may be substituted by well-drained spinach)

Mary Gordon, Edinburgh North F.G.

---

37   # MACARONI BURGERS

1 oz. Polyunsaturated marg.	2 oz. broken macaroni (cooked)
20 blended peanuts	2 oz. cheese (grated)
sage, nutmeg seasoning	
½ beaten egg	2 tbsp. brown flour

Mix the macaroni and peanuts, then add the cheese and seasonings. Add the egg and flour. Shape into rounds and fry in marg. Leave in the fridge if possible.

Makes 3 - 4

Mary Robins, Glasgow

4 oz. wholewheat macaroni	1 large onion, peeled and chopped
1 tbsp. oil	4 oz. mushrooms, washed and sliced
8 oz tomatoes (fresh or tinned)	1 egg, beaten
6 oz. grated cheese	Salt and black pepper

Set oven to 190°C or Mark 5.

Cook macaroni and drain. Fry onion in oil till cooked, but not brown. Add the mushrooms and tomatoes, and cook for 5 mins. Remove from heat, add the macaroni, 4oz. of the cheese and the beaten egg. Taste and season. Pour into a shallow ovenproof dish and sprinkle the remaining 2oz. of cheese on top. Bake 25 - 30 mins. until hot and bubbling on the top.

Freezes well

Molly Hood, Glasgow West F.G.

HINTS

Cheesecrumb Casserole Topping

(Can be made in blender or mixer)

Roughly cube old cheese, crusts, bits of bread.

Add them together in small lots in blender or mixer and reduce to crumb consistency.

Use as crispy cheese topping for casseroles, and store spare portions in marg. tubs in your freezer for handy use at any time.

If cheese or bread is fresh, add a little oatmeal to ensure dry, not gluey cheesecrumbs.

Valerie Yule, Aberdeen

39   BEAN CAKES (GAMBIA)

110 g. beans (black eyed or butter beans)	1 onion, chopped
110 g. shredded spinach	1 tomato, chopped
Salt, pepper, cayenne and ground garlic	2 eggs
Oil	

Soak the beans overnight, rinse them under cold water and then skin by rubbing them through your hands. Cook the beans till tender (about an hour). Grind the beans, add the onion, tomato, spinach and seasoning and mix well. Beat the eggs and mix all to a thick batter. Grease some small tins (an egg poacher is ideal) and put over boiling water. Spoon in the batter and cook with the lid closed for about 30 mins. or till set.

Liz Paterson, Airdrie

40   BEAN TOMATO STEW

8oz. uncooked soya beans and kidney beans

3 onions	3 stalks celery
1 clove garlic	5 oz. tomato pureé
1 pt. water	1 tsp. salt
$\frac{1}{4}$ tsp. each of cinnamon, nutmeg, cloves and all spice	
4 oz. grated cheddar cheese	$\frac{1}{2}$ tsp. ground cummin
1 green pepper	

1. Soak the beans overnight in water.
2. Boil for $1\frac{1}{2}$ to 2 hrs. until soft.
3. Peel and chop onion, chop celery.
4. Combine all the other ingredients except the cheese and the pepper in a pan.
5. Cook over a low heat for $\frac{1}{2}$ hr.
6. Add the cheese and chopped pepper and remove from stove.
   The residual heat will warm through the pepper and melt the cheese.

serves 4

Iona Wallace, Greenock F.G.

41 HOT CRUSTY BAKED BEANS

Crust: 4 oz. flour (wholemeal)   ½ tsp. salt
        ½ tsp. baking powder   2 oz. marg.
        3 tbsp. dried milk   1 egg

Mix together with enough water to make a pancake-like consistency. May
be slightly lumpy. Spread thinly on bottom and sides of a large
casserole dish.

Filling: 12 oz. mince or sausages   1 large chopped onion
         1 tsp. salt   1 tsp. chili powder
         ½ tsp. tabasco sauce (optional) 1 tin tomatoes
         2 cups undrained cooked kidney beans or one 14 oz. tin

Brown the mince and onion. Add the remaining ingredients. Spoon into
crust and bake @ 350°F for 30 mins. Serve with a green salad and brown
bread or rice.

Serves 6

Sue Pattison, Glasgow South F.G.

42 CURRIED RICE AND CHICK PEA RING

8 oz. long grain rice   ¾ pt. of water
1 tsp. salt   2 large onions
4 - 6 tsp. curry powder   2 apples
2 bananas   juice of ½ lemon
4 oz. raisins   6 - 8 tbsp. mayonnaise
                8 oz. chick peas

Boil the rice for 45 mins. Fry the onion for 10 mins. with the curry
powder, and add half to the cooked rice. Peel and dice the apples and
bananas and toss in lemon juice, add to rice with the raisins. Season
to taste. Press into an oiled 2 pt. ring mould or pile round the edge
of a flan dish, leaving space in the centre for the filling. Stir the
remaining onion and curry into the mayonnaise and then add the cooked
chick peas. Pile into the centre. Garnish with red pepper and parsley.

Roslyn Scott, Kilmallie, Fort William, Lochaber F.G.

(A Middle Eastern dish -- delicious with salad or as a dip
or as a 'starter' spread on crackers or on baked potatoes)

8 oz. cooked chick peas	1 clove garlic - crushed
2 tbsp. oil (olive if possible)	2 tbsp. lemon juice
1 tbsp. sesame seeds or tahini (sesame paste)	
1 tsp. paprika	salt and pepper

Liquidise the chick peas and garlic with a little of the cooking
liquid - just enough to allow the blender to do its job smoothly! Add
the other ingredients and blend again - adjust the flavour with more
lemon juice if wanted. Chill and serve sprinkled with paprika and
chopped parsley.

Win Kennedy, South Midlands F.G.

44   KIDNEY BEAN SAVOURY

¼ lb. kidney beans (soaked and cooked)
   or (if in a hurry) a medium sized tin will do
10 fl. oz. carton sour cream   4 courgettes
Sprig of fresh rosemary (optional)   1 small onion

Sweat sliced courgettes and onion in a small amount of low fat oil or
marg. along with the optional rosemary. Mix with the cooked beans and
sour cream. Top with bread crumbs. Bake in a low oven for 10 mins. or
¼ hr. if ingredients have cooled. Prown under grill.

Serves 4 as main dish with green salad and warmed brown bread.

Chris McGregor, Edinburgh South F.G.

LENTIL BAKE

12 oz. lentils
(brown or green, soaked, cooked until tender, strained)

2 onions, chopped	1 carrot, grated
2 eggs, beaten	1 tsp. veg. oil
1 tsp. mixed herbs	1 tsp. ground ginger
1 tsp. brewer's (dried) yeast (optional)	
1 tsp. vegan or marmite	Sea salt and black pepper
Oil to fry onions (tbsp.)	Tomato puree

Grated cheese for topping if desired

Heat the oil in a medium to large saucepan. Fry the onions for 5 mins. Add the grated carrot, lentils, tomato puree, herbs, ginger, veg. extract and the brewer's yeast. Mix in the eggs. Cook for 10 mins. over a gentle heat. Season.

Put into an oiled or greased casserole dish, with grated cheese on top if desired. Bake in a medium to hot oven, until brown and crispy, 20 - 30 mins.

Serve with own selection of vegetables and with a sauce if possible. Suggest heated tinned tomatoes, with additions of basil, chopped green or red peppers, garlic if liked, etc.

Jean Charlton, Dumfries & Galloway F.G.

LENTILS AND EGGS

2 oz. of green lentils per person

Cover the lentils with salted water approx. 1" above the level of the lentils. Boil, stirring occasionally, till all the water is absorbed. Flavour if liked with yoghurt or ketchups or any preferred flavouring. (You can also cook onion with the lentils if wished).

Serve with boiled, poached or fried eggs (1 each).

Lisbett Rutter, Edinburgh

(Quick to make, especially if you keep a supply of ground nuts ready)
(Children like it)

For each person take:

2 oz. ground peanuts	1 oz. oatmeal
1 oz. wholewheat breadcrumbs	½ a small onion, chopped

Fry together in ½ oz. of vegetable marg. for 5 mins. Add tomato puree and/or yeast extract, salt and pepper to taste and enough stock to give the desired fairly soft consistency. Simmer very gently for 15 mins. making sure that it doesn't get too dry.

Serve with a border of mashed potatoes and a green vegetable.

Left over nut mince can easily be used to make rissoles or to stuff vegetables such as green peppers or aubergines.

Win Kennedy, South Midlands F.G.

48   SAMBAR (SOUTH INDIA)

Part 1: 1 cup green or yellow lentils (dal)   2 tsp. salt
         1 qt. water   1 tsp. coriander
         ½ tsp. tumeric   ½ tsp. chilli pepper
         ½ tsp. cummin   1 tbsp. lemon juice

Part 2: Fry in 2 tbsp. oil: 1 tsp. mustard seeds
                            2 tsp. unsweetened grated coconut

Part 3: About 1 cup of any 2 of the following vegetables cut in large chunks:
         Green tomatoes   Green pepper
         Brinjal (egg plants)   Chou-chou (like turnip)

Part 4: 1 - 2 tsp. Sambar powder

1. Clean and soak the dal for about 15 mins. in 1 qt. water. Cook about 15 mins. in same water adding spices listed in Part 1.

2. In a small frypan, brown mustard seeds and coconut and add to above.

3. Add the chopped vegetables. Cook 10 - 15 mins until dal is soft and vegetables are cooked.

4. Add sambar powder, simmer 2 - 3 mins., then remove from the heat and put into a serving dish. Serve with boiled rice.

Serves 4
Dorothy and Peter Millar, Madras, India, (Glasgow Central F.G.)   **29**

49   SWEET AND SOUR SOYBEANS

2 tbsp. veg. oil	6 cups cooked soybeans
2 tins tomatoes	¼ cup brown sugar
¼ cup vinegar	3 large carrots, sliced ¼"
1 large tin unsweetened pineapple	6 tbsp. soy sauce
1 lb. onions, sliced	4 cloves garlic
¼ tbsp. ground ginger (or fresh)	3 tbsp. cornflour
1 green pepper (optional)	

Combine in a bowl the cornflour, sugar, ginger, soy sauce, vinegar and pineapple juice.

Heat in a pan or wok the oil and add the onion, (pepper), carrots and garlic. Stir fry for 3 mins. and then add the soybeans (drained), the pineapple chunks and the tomatoes. Fry for 2 mins., then add the sauce. Cook and stir until the mixture boils (about 2 mins.).

Serve over hot rice.

Serves 10 - 12

Alan and Lorraine Pratt, King's Park, Glasgow

50   WHOLEWHEAT SPAGHETTI AND LENTILS

8 oz. spaghetti

Sauce:	1 onion, chopped	1 red pepper, chopped
	1 clove garlic	1 small can tomatoes
	4 oz. split red lentils	1 tbsp. tomato puree
	¼ pt. water	

Topping: Grated cheddar or parmesan cheese

Sauce: Fry onion and pepper in a little oil in a large pan for 5 mins. Add the other ingredients. Bring to the boil and leave to simmer for 20 mins. Season to taste with salt and pepper.

Cook spaghetti in a large pan, half full of boiling water, for 10 - 15 mins. Drain.

Serve spaghetti with the sauce, topped with cheese.

Serves 4

Mary Gordon, Edinburgh North F.G.

51　BREAD AND BUTTER PIZZA

4 (approx) slices wholemeal bread, buttered
1 egg, beaten　　　　　　　8 fl. oz. skimmed milk
15 oz. tin chopped tomatoes　　1 large onion, chopped
4 oz. grated cheddar cheese

Cover base of a large ovenproof dish with buttered slices of bread. Pour over the beaten egg and milk and allow to soak in. Top with tomatoes, onion and cheese.

Cook in a moderately hot oven for 30 mins.

Mary Gordon, Edinburgh North F.G.

52　BULGAR SAVOURY

8 oz. bulgar　　　　　　　2 carrots
1 onion　　　　　　　　1 tbsp. sultanas
3 tbsp. natural orange juice
Small amount of any green veg. you have: (e.g. celery, spring onion green stalks - if using instead of onion, broccoli sprigs)
2 tbsp. nuts (any except salted variety)

Soak the sultanas in the orange juice while preparing the other ingredients. Sweat the vegetables in a low fat marg. or oil (small amount) till soft. Boil bulgar for 2 mins. Drain, then mix with the vegs. and sultanas. Salt and pepper to taste. Top with wholemeal bread crumbs. Bake for about 10 mins. in a moderate oven and/or brown under a grill.

Serve with green salad as main dish for 4 or as an accompaniment for 6

Chris McGregor, Edinburgh South F.G.

53   DANISH FRITTERS

Make a thick batter, add a can of drained sweetcorn and a small amount
of left over meat or vegs. to taste.

Fry in corn oil in dollops!

Kate McIlhagga, Cambridge/Northants F.G.

54   PASTA WITH TOMATO

(Best next day!)

Pasta: 4 oz. per hungry eater!

Sauce (enough for 6 - 8 portions):

Cooking oil	Garlic granules
½ green pepper, finely chopped	2 tins plum tomatoes
1 tsp. salt	Pinch basil or marjoram
Black or hot red pepper	Parmesan cheese

Cover the bottom of a heavy-based pan with cooking oil, and when hot
add a sprinkle or two of garlic granules, and about ½ a green pepper
chopped fairly finely. Stir until well coated, lower heat and with lid
on cook <u>very</u> gently until soft (not burned!). Add two tins of plum
tomatoes, and use the potato masher when they are soft enough, or put
through a "mouli" before adding to the dish. Add about 1 tsp. salt, a
pinch of basil or marjoram and black or hot red pepper. Cook very
gently, lid-less, either in the oven at the bottom as something else
cooks slowly, or very low heat on the top, for about one hour - should
be fairly thick consistency.

Next day, or day after, re-heat the sauce gently as you cook the pasta
as usual in plenty of boiling salted water until soft enough. Then
pour on a cupful of cold water before draining and dishing up the
pasta with the sauce and a sprinkle of parmesan cheese on top, or
follow with cheese and green salad and bread.

                          Violet Ross, Tayside F.G.

(This pizza is made with a scone base and is <u>very</u> popular in our family. I usually make it when I am making scones, just setting aside enough scone dough to spread over the base of whatever size tin I need, and baking the rest of the dough as scones separately, but at the same time, in the oven)

Wholewheat scone mixture:

8 oz. wholewheat flour	4 oz. plain flour
1½ tsp. baking soda	1½ tsp. cream of tartar
1 tsp. salt	1 small piece marg.
1 tsp. syrup	¼ pt. sour milk (approx.)

Filling:

2 onions, chopped	1 clove crushed garlic
1 tin tomatoes	Salt and pepper
1 tsp. oregano	Bacon or mushrooms (optional)

Topping: Grated cheese

Scone mixture: Mix together the wholewheat flour, plain flour, baking soda, cream of tartar and salt. Rub in the marg., mix in the syrup, and add about ¼ pt. sour milk to mix to a fairly stiff consistency. Spread some dough in the pizza tin, roll out the rest and cut out scones.

Filling: Have this ready to put on top of the dough. Chop and fry the onions with the clove of crushed garlic. Mash and add the tomatoes. Season with the salt, pepper and oregano. (Chopped fried bacon can also be added to the mixture, or mushrooms, if liked).

Spread filling on the dough, sprinkle generously with grated cheese and bake in a hot oven (400°F) for 20 mins. until brown on top.

<u>Hint</u> – Set the tin on a baking tray as it tends to bubble over.

Serve with baked potatoes, if very hungry, and a green salad.

Win Kennedy, South Midlands F.G.

2 oz. brown or white rice per person
Tinned or fresh tomatoes   Grated cheese
Onions and herbs (optional)

Cook the rice with salted water up to 1" above the rice. Cover with a lid, bring to fast boil then simmer. For white rice allow 10 - 15 mins.; for brown (THAI or SURINAM) rice allow 30 mins. Other kinds of brown rice vary. Do not open the lid before time - if all water is not absorbed (better to use too much water than too little) drain and use as/with soups stock.

Add tinned (drained) or fresh tomatoes and grated cheese. (Onions and herbs can be cooked with the rice if wished). For variety add tinned or smoked fish instead of the cheese.

Lisbet Rutter, Edinburgh

57   VEGETABLE RICE - MADRAS

(Quantities of spices and vegetables can be adjusted
according to taste and requirement)

2½ cups rice		4 onions, chopped
3 large tomatoes, chopped	OR	14 oz. tin chopped tomatoes
1 or 2 cups semicooked mixed veg.		3 tbsp. dessic. coconut
1 garlic pip		1 sq. in. root ginger, chopped
3 cloves		3 cardamom
1 level tsp. chilli powder	OR	6 green chillies
1 level tsp. turmeric		1 dssp. poppy seed
1 tsp. coriander powder		¼" cinnamon stick

2½ tsp. salt

Fry the onions until just soft. Add the coconut and all the spices. Fry gently, turning until the onions and spices are well blended. Add the chopped tomatoes and fry for a min. or two. Add the rice - fry for 3 or 4 mins. until the grains are opaque. Add 5 cups of boiling water and salt, simmer. After about 10 mins., when the rice is half-cooked, add the vegetable and cook for a further 10 mins. or so, until all the liquid is absorbed.

Serve with plain yoghurt, and banana, tomato or cucumber side dishes. This is an adequate and tasty meal. To increase the protein intake, a lentil 'stew' or sambar can be served with it.

Anne MacKenzie, Pennine F.G.

58   ## FOUR BEAN SALAD

```
3 rounded tbsp. mayonnaise
1 rounded tbsp. crunchy peanut butter
1 tbsp. milk
1 lb. (450g.) broad beans, shelled and cooked
15¼ oz. (432 g.) can red kidney beans (drained)
14 oz. (400 g.) can white kidney beans (drained)
6 oz. (150 g.) bean sprouts.
```

Mix mayonnaise, peanut butter and milk in a large bowl. Add beans and bean sprouts and turn to coat.

Morag Boffey, Greenock F.G.

HINT

Bean Salad

Bean salads made with an attractive variety of cooked pulses make a nutritious main dish for summer buffets and, although they may look time consuming to make, I take an easy way out! Every time I cook a bean casserole or stew (I pressure-cook most pulses) I cook 2 - 4 oz. extra to what I need and freeze them in a marg. tub. When I have 3 or 4 varieties in the freezer I can defrost them, add chopped onion/ celery/ tomato/ green pepper/ carrot etc. and a vinaigrette dressing and hey presto! - one bean salad!

Vegetables can vary according to the colours of the beans: I usually use red kidney/ soya/ haricot/ chick pea, and the pale green flageolet beans are also very attractive in salads.

Win Kennedy, South Midlands F.G.

59   ## CHEESE AND HAM SALAD

```
4 oz. cheddar cheese          4 oz. cooked ham
1 small onion                 1 head of celery
4 boiled eggs                 French dressing
some: lettuce, pickles, tomatoes, cucumber, beetroot
```

Dice the ham and cheese neatly. Wash and dice the celery. Chop the onion finely. Wash and dry the lettuce. Hard boil the eggs. Add the other ingredients when ready to serve and finally the French dressing or salad cream to taste.

Morag Boffey, Greenock F.G.

60   CURRIED PASTA

8 oz. pasta shells or bows   1 tsp. salt
1 tsp. curry powder

Boil pasta as directed on packet. Drain, place in a bowl and add salad
cream. Mix with the tsp. of curry powder.

Leave to cool, decorate with tomato wedges.

Morag Boffey, Greenock F.G.

61   STUFFED CELERY

1 head celery   2 oz. cream cheese
1 tbsp. tomato sauce   Cooked meat or fish seasoning
Yolk of hard boiled eggs

Trim the celery and separate the stalks. Beat the cheese until soft
and creamy. Add the tomato sauce, finely chopped meat and seasoning.
Stuff grooves of celery with this mixture and sprinkle the tops with
egg yolk finely chopped.

Morag Boffey, Greenock F.G.

62   RICE SALAD

½ lb. long-grained rice, cooked and drained
1 x 11½ oz. can sweet corn, drained
2 celery stalks, chopped
¼ pt. mustard dressing
4 tomatoes, skinned, seeded and chopped.

Put the rice and sweet corn in a large serving bowl and stir to mix.
Stir in the beans, celery, pepper, adding tomatoes last. Pour over the
dressing and fold in carefully. Cover and chill in fridge until
required. Stir before serving.

Morag Boffey, Greenock F.G.

36

8 oz. brown rice	1 garlic clove crushed with a pinch of sea salt
4 tbsp. oil	Freshly ground black pepper
4 oz. peanuts	2 tbsp. cider vinegar
2 oz. raisins	1 tbsp. tamari sauce

1 green pepper, cored, seeded and chopped

Cook the rice in lightly salted boiling water for about 45 mins. or until tender. Drain, rinse with cold water and drain again. Beat together the oil, vinegar, tamari sauce, garlic and pepper. Mix the dressing into rice. Leave rice to cool. Mix in the peanuts, pepper and raisins. Leave the salad for 15 mins. before serving.

Emma Roberton, Glasgow South F.G.

64   LIGHT LUNCH SALAD

(serves 4)

2 apples	2 pears
1 orange	1 banana
8 oz. cottage cheese	Lettuce

Chopped nuts

Prepare and chop the fruits. Mix with the cottage cheese. Serve on a bed of lettuce. Garnish with the nuts.

Mary Gordon, Edinburgh North F.G.

HINT

Cheap Winter Salad

Grate roughly equal amounts of apple and carrot and mix well.

Herbs, small amounts of chopped celery or grated orange rind can be added for variety.

Lisbett Rutter, Edinburgh

65   TABBOULEH

(Another Middle Eastern dish - very refreshing in summmer
and <u>very</u> easy to make - no cooking!)

8 oz. bulgur wheat (this is cracked, pre-cooked wheat,
      which is available in wholefood shops)
1 bunch spring onions
3 - 4 tomatoes
Parsley and Mint - a generous handful of each :-
      (1 tbsp. of dried mint can be used if fresh mint is not
      available, but fresh is <u>much</u> better)
3 tbsp. vegetable oil (olive is traditional)
2 tbsp. lemon juice
Salt and pepper

Put the wheat in a bowl and cover with water to 1 inch above wheat.
Leave to soak for an hour, until the wheat has swollen and absorbed
some of the water. (I usually do my soaking overnight, so I'm not sure
quite how long it takes!)

Drain, put the soaked wheat in a sieve, and squeeze out any remaining
water with the back of a large spoon. Transfer to a salad bowl, add
the chopped spring onions, roughly chopped tomatoes, and the finely
chopped parsley and mint. Mix well, add the oil, juice and seasoning -
adjust to taste. (I usually add more lemon juice).

Serve on crisp lettuce as a refreshingly different salad.

Win Kennedy, South Midlands F.G.

66   TOMATO MOULD

4 Tomatoes or half a tin	3 hard boiled eggs
1 tsp. bread crumbs	1 large tbsp. cornflour
1 oz. butter (or margarine)	½ tsp. mace (or mixed herbs)

Pepper and salt to taste

Cook the tomatoes in the butter (or marg.). Mix the cornflour with a
teacupful of milk or, if tinnned tomatoes are used, the liquid from
the tin. Add this to the cooked tomatoes. Cook for 5 mins. Add the
eggs chopped up finely, and then the breadcrumbs. Pour into a mould.
Turn out when cold.

Serve with salad and mayonnaise.

Runa Mackay, Edinburgh Central F.G.

67   FUMPH

> 1 packet of marshmallows
> 1 tin mandarins
> 1 tin pineapple chunks
> Small carton double cream (or large if preferred)

Wet scissors, then cut marshmallows into quarters. Soak in the fruit juice for 1 hour. Add the mandarins and pineapple, well strained. Fold in whipped double cream.

Anonymous, Kings Park Church, Glasgow.

68   LEMON PUDDING

> Juice and rind of a good-sized lemon
> ¼ pt. water   4 ozs. sugar
> 1 egg - separated   1½ tbsp. cornflour

Bring juice and rind of lemon, water and sugar to the boil. Mix yolk of egg with cornflour and a little cold water. Add to the mixture. Bring back to boil and pour into a casserole dish. Beat up white of egg until stiff and fold into the mixture.

Margaret M. McLagan, King's Park Church, Glasgow.

69   ORANGE SOUFFLÉ

> 6 ozs. sugar   3 eggs
> Juice of 2 oranges   Rind of 1 orange
> ½ oz. gelatine

Melt the gelatine in ½ cup of hot water. Cream the egg yolks and sugar. Add orange juice and rind and gelatine and mix. Beat egg whites to a stiff froth. Stir in slowly and pour the mixture into a dish and leave till set.

Runa Mackay, Edinburgh Central F.G.

```
            1 lb. strawberries (can be small, mushy ones or frozen,
                                            when there's a glut)
            1-2 oz. sugar               ¼ pt. orange juice
            ½ oz. gelatine              4 oz. marshmallows
            ¼ pt. double cream          2 egg whites
```

For the sauce: 6 - 8 oz. strawberries   1 oz. icing sugar.

(1) Sieve, mash or liquidise all the strawberries, except for six berries. Add sugar.

(2) Pour orange juice into a basin. Stand over a pan of very hot water. Sprinkle the gelatine on the orange juice and leave until dissolved. Cut marshmallows into small pieces with damp kitchen scissors; add the hot gelatine mixture, leave until melted. Spoon into the strawberry pureé. Allow to stiffen.

(3) Lightly whip the cream. Add almost all of this into the strawberry jelly. Finally fold in the stiffly whisked egg whites.

(4) Spoon into individual dishes/serving dish. Leave until quite firm Make a smooth pureé of the strawberries for the sauce, add sugar, stir until dissolved. Spoon over the mousse and top with the last of the whipped cream and whole strawberries.

<u>Freezing</u> - This freezes well for up to 6 weeks.

Helen Pattison, King's Park Church, Glasgow

HINTS

<u>What's This? Jelly</u>

Dissolve a packet of jelly in sufficient hot water, then top up to one pint with milk - which will curdle it. Strain a little into the bottom of sweets dishes, and leave the rest until it begins to thicken. Whip it up for a minute in the blender, then add to the dishes. Leave in the fridge until ready to serve - or put them in the freezing compartment for 20 mins. until set still fluffy - and add any fruit or decorations you like. Glass dishes are best as they show the jelly set into strata; and the family say, 'What's this?'

<u>Make Your Own Cream</u>

If you get milk in bottles with a little cream on the top, save the cream from four or more bottles and whip in blender for a minute. Leave a while, blend for a minute and repeat a couple of times if it is not thickening. Leave five minutes, then use a knife to pour off any thin milk left underneath the 'fluff', and blend again. If your dairy is any good, you will now have a dish of cream ready to serve.

Valerie Yule, Aberdeen

71 ABBEY CRUNCH BISCUITS

4 ozs. marg.	3 ozs. sugar
4 ozs. S.R. flour	4 tbsp. porage oats
1 tsp. syrup	1 tsp. boiling water

Pinch baking soda

Cream the margarine and sugar. Add the other ingredients. Roll into balls the size of walnuts, flatten slightly. Bake at Reg. 4, 350°F., or 180°C. for about 20 mins.

Margaret M. McLagan, King's Park Church, Glasgow

72 IONA BISCUITS

4 oz. lard	4 oz. marg.
1 dssp. syrup	8 oz. S.R. flour
6 oz. sugar	½ tsp. baking powder

Melt the lard, margarine and syrup in a saucepan. Mix together the flour, sugar and baking powder and add to the melted mixture in the pan. Place balls of the mixture on a greased baking tray. Press down (once) with a fork.

Bake at 300°F for 7 - 10 mins.

Jessie Thompson, King's Park Church, Glasgow

73 IONA BISCUITS (CATERING SIZE)

2 lb. marg.	8 dssp. syrup
3 lb. S.R. flour	4 tsp. baking powder
1½ lb. sugar	Flavouring

Melt the margarine and syrup in a pan. Mix the other ingredients well and add to the melted mixture. Add flavouring if desired. Roll the mixture into balls and place on oiled trays. Flatten with a fork.

Bake in an oven @ Gas mark 3 - 4 for 7 - 10 mins. till golden brown. Cool on wire trays.

Coffee House, Iona

74   IONA BISCUIT FUDGE

8 oz. marg.	4 oz. sugar
1 egg	1 tbsp. drinking chocolate
Biscuit or cake crumbs	Cooking chocolate to cover

Melt together the marg., sugar and drinking chocolate in a saucepan. Add enough biscuit or cake crumbs to make a fairly dry mixture. Add the raw egg to bind. Press into two trays. Cover with cooking chocolate.

Jessie Thompson, King's Park Church, Glasgow

(Good, quick and easy - makes a huge cake which everyone enjoys)

3 cups plain flour (you can substitute some of this with brown
flour, or just add ½ cup of brown)

2 cups brown sugar	2 tsp. bicarbonate of soda
6 tbsp. cocoa	1 tsp. salt
2 tsp. vanilla essence	¼ cup corn oil
4 tbsp. vinegar	2 cups water

Place in a large bowl the flour, sugar, bicarbonate of soda, cocoa and salt. Add the vanilla essence, corn oil, vinegar and water. Mix well together. Place in a large oblong roasting-type tin. Cook @ Gas mark 4 for 35 to 40 mins. Leave to cool.

Mix some icing sugar, cocoa (tsp. coffee powder) with water to form a stiffish paste. Place over the surface and smooth down. Cut into chunks - irresistable!

Ruth Shanks, Edinburgh South F.G.

76 MILLIONAIRE SHORTBREAD (CATERING SIZE)

Base:	1 lb. marg.		8 oz. sugar
	Pinch salt		2 lb. flour
		A little water	

Toffee:	1 lb. marg.		1 lb. sugar
	8 tbsp. syrup		2 tins condensed milk

Topping: 24 oz. melted chocolate

Base: Cream the marg. and sugar. Add the flour and salt. Mix till it forms a dough - adding a little water to make it doughier. Roll onto a very large oiled and floured tray. Prick with a fork and bake @ Gas mark 4 - 5 till light golden.

Toffee: Melt all the ingredients in a pan. Bring to the boil, stirring all the time. Continue to boil and stir the mixture until it darkens to toffee - 10 mins approx. Spread onto the base.

Topping: Melt the chocolate in a metal dish over a pan of hot water and spread over the toffee.

Coffee House, Iona

77   MUESLI BISCUITS

4 oz. polyunsaturated marg.	1 tbsp. golden syrup
2 oz. soft brown sugar	3 oz. muesli
3 oz. wholewheat flour	

Heat oven to 325°F, Gas mark 3.   Use 2 large baking sheets.

Put the marg. and sugar into a small saucepan – heat gently until the marg. has melted. Mix the sugar, flour and muesli in a bowl, then stir into the melted mixture and blend thoroughly.

Spoon teaspoons of the mixture onto the sheets – leaving room for expansion. Bake for 20 mins. until golden brown. Allow to cool for a few mins., then lift off with a palette knife.

Finish cooling on a cake rack.

Makes 20 approx.

Mary Robins, Glasgow

78   YOUTH CAMP OATCAKES

150 g. oatmeal	50 g. flour
50 g. marg.	¼ tsp. salt
Pinch baking soda	

Mix the dry ingredients and rub in the fat. Mix with warm water to a stiff consistency and turn out on to a surface sprinkled with oatmeal. Roll and cut out.

Cook @ 150°C, No.2 for 45 mins.

Liz Paterson, Airdrie

(This recipe comes originally from Canada. It was the first recipe my mother ever made up, and also the first one I was let loose on. The only thing that you can do wrong is to burn the biscuits! The dough tastes good before you bake it, and just rolls and rolls, and even when it gets dry doesn't affect the end result of the biscuits. The biscuits are good on their own but especially delicious with cheese)

3 teacups flour	$\frac{1}{4}$ lb. butter (or marge)
3 teacups oatmeal	1 tsp. salt
2 teacups brown sugar	1 - 2 tsp. cinnamon
$\frac{1}{4}$ cup milk (sour)	1 tsp. baking soda

Dissolve the baking soda in the milk and melt the butter (or marge). Mix the dry ingredients. Add the melted butter and the baking soda in milk. Firm dough. Roll out fairly thin and cut in rounds.

Bake on a greased tray in a moderate oven for about 30 mins. or until ready.

Catherine Hepburn, Central F.G.

80 SHORTBREAD

Scottish Shortbread

9 oz. plain flour
3 oz. cornflour
3 oz. castor sugar
Pinch of baking powder
$\frac{1}{4}$ lb. butter

Melt the butter and then add all the other ingredients.

Spread into a swiss roll tin. Mark with a fork and bake @ Reg 4, 350°F or 180°C for $\frac{1}{4}$ - $\frac{1}{2}$ hour, until brown.

Sprinkle with sugar and mark while still hot.

Margaret M. McLagan,
King's Park Church, Glasgow

81   DATE SQUARES

8 oz. chopped dates   4 tbsp. lemon juice
¼ tsp. cinnamon   6 oz. marg.
2 oz. golden syrup   8 oz. rolled oats
4 oz. wholemeal flour   4 oz. soft brown sugar

Cook the dates, lemon juice and cinnamon in a small pan for 5 mins.

Heat the marg. and syrup in another pan till melted. Stir in the oats,
sugar and flour. Mix well. Press half the oats mixture into a 7"
square tin. Spread the date mixture over it. Top with the remaining
oats and press down well.

Cook @ Gas mark 4, 350°F, for 20 mins.

Cool for 5 mins., then cut into squares.   Makes 16

                    Cristine Ferguson, Glasgow Central F.G.

82   FLAPJACKS

    200 g. marg.   200 g. flour
    120 g. brown sugar   140 g. oatflakes

Cut the marg. into the flour and by finger add the brown sugar and
oats. Press into a flat grease-papered tin. Leave in a cool place for
half an hour.

Bake until brown (lightish) in a fairly hot oven.

                    Runa Mackay, Edinburgh Central F.G.

83   MELTING MOMENTS

    Crushed cornflakes   4 oz. marg.
    3 oz. sugar   1 egg yolk
                    6 oz. S.R. flour

Cream the butter and sugar. Beat in the egg yolk. Blend in the flour
and mix to a smooth paste. Divide into portions the size of a walnut.
Roll in the crushed cornflakes.

Place on a greased baking sheet and bake @ 375°F, Gas 5, for 12 mins.

                    Ella Ferguson, King's Park Church, Glasgow

(If you have never tried carrots in a cake, don't be put off! It is quite delicious, moist and sweet and spicy. This recipe is supposed to keep well, but in my house it disappears very fast!)

Butter mixture:

      1½ cups (12 oz.) melted butter   1¾ cups brown sugar
      4 eggs at room temperature   Grated rind of one lemon

Beat together in a large bowl, beginning with the butter and sugar. Add the eggs one at a time. Add the lemon rind and beat until light in colour.

Flour mixture - sift together twice:

      2 cups wholemeal flour   2 cups white flour
      1 tsp. salt   ½ tsp. bicarbonate of soda
      3 tsp. baking powder   1 tsp. ground allspice
                2 tsp. ground ginger

Carrots:

   2½ cups grated raw carrot (about 2 - 3 large carrots) soaked in the juice of the lemon.

Nuts and fruit:

   1½ cups mixed raisins, nuts, dried apricots - whatever you have available

Add the flour mixture and spoonfuls of grated carrot to the butter mixture, mixing gently after each addition. Do not beat. Add nuts and fruit last.

Butter a large cake tin and sprinkle it with poppy seeds. Put in the cake mixture and bake for about an hour @ 350°F. Cool in the tin for 10 mins. before turning out onto a rack.

The carrot cake will be sprinkled with the poppy seeds and doesn't need icing, but is delicious split and sandwiched together with a filling made of one part unsalted butter to three parts cream cheese.

                                     Marion McNaughton, Leeds

85 FRUIT LOAF

1 cup milk	1 cup fruit
1 cup sugar	¼ lb. marg.
2 cups plain flour	½ tsp. baking soda
½ tsp. baking powder	1 small egg, beaten

Melt in a pan the milk, fruit, sugar and marg. and leave to cool. Pour the melted mixture into a bowl containing the flour, baking soda, baking powder and the egg and mix well.

Divide the mixture between two 1 lb. loaf tins, greased, floured, sprinkled with a little sugar and the bottoms of the tins covered with greaseproof paper.

Bake for one hour at Reg. 4, 350°F or 180°C.

Margaret M. McLagan, King's Park Church, Glasgow

86 MANSE CAKE- CATERING SIZE

3 lb. sugar	6 tbsp. treacle
3 lb. raisins	1½ lb. marg.
3 pt. water	12 tsp. baking powder
4½ lb. S.R. flour	6 eggs
3 tsp. each mixed spice, cinnamon, ginger	

Boil everything except the flour, baking powder and eggs for 3 mins. in a large pot. Cool the mixture and add remaining ingredients.

Place in greased, lined tins (use marg. wrappers).

Bake @ Gas. 4 for 1 to 1½ hours.

Remove from the tins and cool on racks.   Slice only when cool.

Coffee House, Iona

```
6 oz. (175 g.) butter or marg.        3 eggs, beaten
6 oz. (175 g.) golden gran. sugar     2 tbsp. milk
6 oz. (175 g.) wholemeal flour, sifted  2½ level tsp. baking powder
1 oz. (25 g.) chopped hazelnuts    4 oz. (110 g.) ground hazelnuts
      7 oz. (200 g.) plain dessert chocolate, chopped quite small
```

Pre-heat the oven to Gas mark 4, 350°F (180°C)
You will need a 7 inch (18cm) greased and lined, deep, round cake tin

First, cream together the butter and sugar until pale, light and
fluffy. Then add the eggs, a little at a time, beating well between
each addition. Now fold in the milk, sifted flour and baking powder
and fold and mix them well. Now add the chocolate pieces together with
the ground hazelnuts and then spoon the mixture into the prepared
tin.
Finally, sprinkle over the chopped hazelnuts and bake the cake in the
centre of the oven for about 1½ hours or until the centre is springy
when lightly touched. After one hour cover cake with a sheet of
greaseproof paper, to prevent the nuts over-browning. Leave to cool
in the tin for 5 - 10 mins. before turning out.

Makes 12 - 16 slices

Molly Harvey, Glasgow Central F.G.

HINTS

Orange Refrigerator Cookies

```
10 oz. plain flour.    1 tsp. baking powder.   5 oz. butter or marg.
6 oz. castor sugar.    2 tsp. grated orange rind.   2 oz. currants
   1 large egg, lightly beaten.    Extra sugar for dusting.
```

Sieve together the flour and baking powder. Cream the butter, sugar
and rind of orange until light and fluffy. Beat in the egg. Stir in
the currants and the flour until the mixture clings together. Turn on
to a lightly floured surface and form into sausage shapes - about 2"
diameter. Wrap in foil or waxed paper and chill in fridge or freezer.
To cook, thinly slice off as many as you need and place on a greased
tray - sprinkle with sugar. Bake at Reg.4, 350°F, 180°C, for 15 mins.
Cool on the trays for 2 mins., then transfer to a wire rack. Makes 48
biscuits.

Bran Loaf

1 cup each: Soft brown sugar, sultanas, allbran, milk, S.R.flour.

Mix the sugar, sultanas and allbran with the milk and leave
overnight.
Next morning add the flour and bake for 1 hour @ Reg.5, 375°F, 190°C.

Margaret M. McLagan, King's Park Church, Glasgow   **49**

88   EASY FUDGE/TABLET

2/3 cup milk
1 tsp. vanilla
1 tbsp. butter
2 oz. chocolate

Heat the sugar, butter and milk to boiling point. Add the chocolate and stir until melted. Boil 13 mins. (exactly). Remove from heat. Add the vanilla and beat until the mixture is creamy and sugary around the edge of the pan. Pour into buttered pans. When cooled slightly, mark into squares.

Runa Mackay, Edinburgh Central F.G.

89   LEMON AND APPLE JAM

3 lemons   4½lb. sugar   2¼ pt. cold water
2 lb. cooking apples (weighed after peeling etc.)

Wash and slice the lemons. Put in a bowl with 2 pts. of the water. Put the pips in another bowl with the remaining ¼ pt. of water. Leave for 24 hours.

Peel, core and slice the apples, then weigh. Put in a preserving pan. Put the lemons and their liquid through a mincer or liquidiser and add to the pan. Strain the jelly from the pips and add also.

Bring to the boil then boil for 20 mins. After which add the sugar. Stir well till the sugar is dissolved, and return to the boiling point and again boil briskly till the jam sets. Setting or jelling usually takes 20 - 30 mins.

Chris Mitchell, Glasgow South F.G.

¼ lb. tomatoes	1 oz. butter
1 small onion	1 egg
2 oz. fine white bread crumbs	1 oz. grated cheese

Salt and pepper to taste

Drop the tomatoes into boiling water for 1 min. Remove skins and chop, then put them in a pan with the butter. Add the onion, finely chopped or grated, the egg well beaten, and seasoning. Stir gently over a low heat till beginning to thicken, then remove from the heat. Add the breadcrumbs and grated cheese. Heat once more till well mixed.

Put into small pots, pour a little melted butter on top to seal.

Chris Mitchell, Glasgow South F.G.

HINT

Lemonade

Makes 3½ pts. concentrated juice.

3 lemons   3 lb. sugar   2 pts. boiling water   1 oz. tartaric acid

Wash, halve and squeeze the lemons. Mince or chop the rinds. Add the sugar and boiling water. Stir. Stand for 24 hours.

Dissolve the tartaric acid in a little hot water and add to the mixture. Stir, strain and bottle.

Runa Mackay, Edinburgh Central F.G.

NOTES

CURRENT PUBLICATIONS OF THE IONA COMMUNITY

SONGS OF THE INCARNATION   ISBN 0 950135186
John Bell & Graham Maule

THE IONA COMMUNITY WORSHIP BOOK   ISBN 0 950135194
Iona Community

THROUGH WOOD AND NAILS   Record No.146/REC/S
Iona Abbey

THROUGH WOOD AND NAILS   Cassette No.IC/WGP/001
Iona Abbey

THE WHOLE EARTH SHALL CRY GLORY   Paperback ISBN 0 947988 00 9
Iona prayers by Rev. George F. MacLeod

THE WHOLE EARTH SHALL CRY GLORY   Hardback ISBN 0 947988 04 1
Iona prayers by Rev. George F. MacLeod

WILD GOOSE PRINTS No.1   ISBN 0 947988 06 8
John Bell & Graham Maule

WHAT IS THE IONA COMMUNITY?   ISBN 0 947988 07 6
Iona Community

WOMEN'S WORDS FROM IONA ABBEY   ISBN 0 947988 08 4
Kathryn Galloway

A TOUCHING PLACE   Cassette No.IC/WGP/004
Wild Goose Worship Group

A TOUCHING PLACE   ISBN 0 947988 09 2
John Bell & Graham Maule

WILD GOOSE PRINTS No.2   ISBN 0 947988 10 6
John Bell & Graham Maule

COLUMBA – The Man & The Myth   ISBN 0 947988 11 4
Mitchell Bunting

IN PRAISE OF GOD'S GOODNESS   ISBN 0 947988 12 2
Kathryn Galloway

THE IONA PILGRIMAGE   ISBN 0 947988 13 0
Jack Kellet

FOLLY AND LOVE   Cassette No.IC/WGP/005
Iona Abbey

FOLLY AND LOVE   ISBN 0 947988 15 7
Iona Abbey

SINGING THE SACRAMENT   ISBN 0 947988 16 5
John Bell

90 RECIPES FROM THE IONA COMMUNITY   ISBN 0 947988 17 3
Sue Pattison

GRACE AND DYSENTERY   ISBN 0 947988 19 X
Ron Ferguson

EH…JESUS…YES, PETER…?   ISBN 0 947988 20 3
John Bell & Graham Maule

FREEDOM IS COMING   Cassette No.IC/WGP/006
Utryck

FREEDOM IS COMING   ISBN 91 86788 15 7
Utryck

CLOTH FOR THE CRADLE   Cassette No.IC/WGP/007
Wild Goose Worship Group

AT GROUND LEVEL   ISBN 0 947988 21 1
Ruth Burgess & Sally Carlaw

CO-OPERATION VERSUS EXPLOITATION   ISBN 0 947988 22 X
Walter Fyfe

WILD GOOSE SONGS – VOLUME 1   ISBN 0 947988 23 8
John Bell & Graham Maule

53

BOOKS

THE WHOLE EARTH SHALL CRY GLORY
Iona prayers by Rev. George F. MacLeod

These prayers by the founder of the Iona Community (now Very Rev. Lord MacLeod of Fuinary) are drawn from the whole period of his leadership of worship in the Community. "The language of the prayers is evocative of the Celtic mysticism of Columban Iona. The profound spirituality, linked with deep reverence for the earth and the common things of life, so characteristic of Celtic Christianity, are reflected here; so also is the rich, imaginative language and unexpected phrase which lights up another aspect of the world." The prayers are accompanied by over twenty full colour photographs, taken by members or staff of the Community, which serve as an aid to meditation.

| £2.95 | Paperback – ISBN 0 947988 01 7 |
| £4.95 | Hardback – ISBN 0 947988 04 1 |

IONA COMMUNITY WORSHIP BOOK

This book includes many services of Worship by the Community in Iona Abbey and places where members gather, including 'Columban Houses' and Family Groups. The Worship is rich and varied, drawing on a long and wide tradition with much new material. There are new songs and hymns, also prayers, old and new, some set to music, in the closing pages of the book.

£1.95   ISBN 0 95013 51 9 4

DRAMA RESOURCES

WILD GOOSE PRINTS No. 1

First of a series of Drama Resource Books, by John Bell and Graham Maule, containing participative material for Worship or discussion, based on the life and teaching of Jesus Christ. "These scripts were written out of the need to enable the Gospel to be communicated through movement, humour and imagination to those who have been turned off by the traditional preaching and evangelism of the church. All have been used and found helpful in youth and mixed age groups and congregations. It is not necessary that those using this material should have any dramatic skill or experience or, indeed, that they should learn everything by he .rt. Several scripts can be effectively used with readers placed in different parts of the same room or hall."

£1.25   ISBN 0 947988 06 8

NEW AT GROUND LEVEL
Poems by Ruth Burgess, Illustrated by Sally Carlaw

These are poems drawn from Ruth Burgess' experience of living and working in inner city areas of Birmingham and London. They tell stories about adults and children, and they reflect an awareness of God in nature and in city streets. Sally Carlaw's pictures sensitively portray and expand the feelings and the questions of the poems.

£1.75   ISBN 0 947988 21 1

WILD GOOSE PRINTS No. 2
Second in the series of Drama Resource Books by John Bell and Graham Maule and the Wild Goose Worship Group. Some of these scripts require more characters and a little more experience to put over well. Also included are a series of discussion starters *Death Conversations* which have been used with good effect as catalysts to conversation on a topic which young people are rarely allowed to explore honestly.

£1.25   ISBN 0 947988 10 6

NEW

EH...JESUS... YES, PETER...?
A new book of Drama scripts by John Bell and Graham Maule containing seven conversations between Jesus and Peter. Using the Gospel record, the authors have constructed the kind of dialogue in which Jesus, speaking to Peter, would reveal his own purpose and remind the eager disciple of his humanity.

£1.25   ISBN 0 947988 20 3

MUSIC

THROUGH WOOD AND NAILS
This recording, produced by Ian and Kathy Galloway, contains many of the new songs from *Songs of the Incarnation* together with prayers and runes, with a service of Morning Worship from the *Community Worship Book*. It was recorded in Iona Abbey. The liveliness of the singing, the quality of the worship, and the atmosphere recorded, are remarkable.

£4.95   Record – 146/REC/S
£4.95   Cassette – IC/WGP/001

SONGS OF THE INCARNATION
A book with 24 new songs and hymns by Rev. John Bell, with graphic illustrations by Graham Maule. Modern and traditional music with lyrics, which have a new depth of meaning, and illustrations which give a new insight and focus for each song. Most of these songs are based on the life of Jesus expressed in contemporary terms.

£2.25   ISBN 0 9501351 8 6

NEW

CLOTH FOR THE CRADLE
The sequel to the cassette *A Touching Place* by the Wild Goose Worship Group, this cassette was produced "to demonstrate the kind of material which can be sung by anyone, but particularly by those for whom the conventional music of the church is failing to speak". There are new religious songs, songs set to traditional folk songs, arrangements of hymns from Central Africa, a meditative chant and, courtesy of the Corrymeela Community, a solo on the Irish whistle.

£3.95   Cassette – IC/WGP/007

FREEDOM IS COMING
Songs of protest and praise from South Africa collected by the Church of Sweden Mission and recorded by Utryck under the editorship and leadership of Anders Nyberg. "Amandala"means power, and certainly there is power in these songs, which were published for the first time in Sweden in 1980 by the song group *Fjedur* and is now marketed in the UK for Utryck by Wild Goose Publications as a cassette and book.

£5.60   Book – ISBN 91 86788 00
£4.90   Cassette – IC/WGP/006

PAMPHLETS

WHAT IS THE IONA COMMUNITY?
A new account of the history of the Iona Community and its rules and current concerns, with a description of its work on both the island of Iona and the Mainland of Great Britain. Information is given as to membership of, and Association with, the Community.

£0.85   ISBN 0 947988 07 6

WOMEN'S WORDS FROM IONA ABBEY
Edited by Kathy Galloway, these songs, meditations and prayers were inspired by the creativity of those taking part in the *Women and the Church* week on Iona. Women, who often felt excluded by the apparent indifference of the church to their skills and experience, worked to discover fresh images and, in discovering, to give them tangible expression.

£0.85   ISBN 0 947988 08 4

COLUMBA – The Man and the Myth
This book , written by Community member Mitchell Bunting, (now Minister of Carrs Lane United Reformed Church, Birmingham) explores the historic record of the life of Columba, separating the man from many of the myths, and revealing something of the dynamism of the man, his people, his times and his faith.

£0.85   ISBN 0 947988 11 4

IN PRAISE OF GOD'S GOODNESS
A book by Kathryn Galloway, joint Warden of Iona Abbey, is a thought provoking meditation on Psalm 107. "The promise is life in all its fullness. Ask and you will receive, seek and you will find, knock and the door will be opened to you." The second part of the book is "a story for everyone who ever felt sorry for the Prodigal Son's elder brother" *Everything That I Have is Yours.* "Somewhere just out of reach, elusive, mysterious, there is a secret for us too".

£0.85   ISBN 0 947988 12 2

THE IONA PILGRIMAGE – One Man's Experience
Jack Kellet has written this excellent book about the Wednesday Pilgrimage around Iona, drawing upon his long experience over many years. The insight which he brings to every step of the way, with meditations at all of the stopping places, make this the ideal companion to take on the pilgrimage, and/or to take home for reflection.

£0.85   ISBN 0 947988 13 0

APOCALYPSE SOON?
Christian Responsibility and the Book of Revelation
A book by Alan E. Lewis published for the Scottish Christian CND, exploring the book of Revelation to discover the Christian's responsibilities in the present situation of nuclear armaments and weapons of mass destruction.

£0.85   ISBN 0 947988 18 1

NEW   **GRACE AND DYSENTERY**
Iona Community Leader Ron Ferguson's experiences of India related by him in a book which explores the contrasts and the immensities of that vast subcontinent and its teeming peoples. "James Cameron it was, I think, who said that if you want to write a book about India, you'd better do it in the first week of your visit. After that, the impressions are so confusing and contradictory that any writer is afflicted by paralysis. I understand. "

£1.25   ISBN 0 947988 19 X